1

DISPLAY ART

Encourage creativity.

Graeme Smith

PUBLISHED ON AMAZON.com
by
LABYRINTH BOOKS

DEDICATION:

This book is dedicated to my family.

    Hele-ly (Ly).

        my wife:

    Ingrid.

        our daughter:

    Marie.

        my former wife:

    Fiona, Natalie and Michael

        our children:

    Georgie

        Michael's wife:

    Pearl, Kiki and Martha.

        their children:

They have put up with me for many years and I thank them for that.
I hope this book is an insight into what occupied me much of the time.
They have all done worthwhile and interesting things.
In the absence of help from me.
I congratulate them for their achievements.

SUPPORT:

Support the International Artist magazine
    contact: editor@internationalartist.com
Support the Australian Artist magazine
    contact: editor@australianartist.com

CREATIVITY.

What is it about?

> **1. The nature of art is considered**
> **2. Linked to that are specific objectives.**
> **3. That's what Display Art introduces!**
> **4. Display Art makes these assumptions.**

1. The nature of art has been considered.

The following are AIMS derived from this analysis.

> To develop the uniqueness of each individual.
> To develop confident self-actualization.
> To develop self-responsibility and initiative.
> To develop creativity and flexibility of thinking.
> To develop visual perceptual ability.

The individual learner develops these qualities:

> Unique person
> Self-actualization
> Self-responsibility
> Creativity
> Perceptual skills

Creativity is a behaviour possessed by all people.

> Even without any teaching.
> But appropriate educational methods can develop it.
> To even higher levels of skill.
> The value of right behaviour is stressed.
> There's interaction of perception, affect and cognition.
> Which is creativity.

1. Display Art provides appropriate strategies.

    To expose students to:

    A creativity nurturing process.

    So creativity skill is developed consequently.

    Strategies are planned, deliberate, sequenced, non-verbal.

2. Related to the above are more specific objectives.

    Skills attitudes concepts are integrated & developed.

    Thus later stages incorporate earlier ones.

    Creativity is a behaviour intrinsic to art and education.

3. This is what SPACE Art Education stood for!

    Structured STIMULUS

        – planned, organized program.

    Perceptual SKILLS

        – developed in response to stimuli.

    Affective ATTITUDES

        – emotion guides student options.

    Cognitive CONCEPTS

        – creative thinking determines action.

    Experiences LEARNING

        – how learning happens.

4. Display Art has identical objectives and assumes:

    1. Creativity is interaction of feeling, thinking doing.

    2. Each learning experience is enjoyable but serious.

    3. A time for student action rather than adult talk.

    4. The student learning experience is self-rewarding.

    5. Each student should work independently.

HOW TO USE THIS BOOK.

Usually people don't think through things to the level needed.
Because of that, they have projects instead of tasks on their "to do" list.
Leading to procrastination as it hasn't been broken down to a task level.
Go through your book once to understand it THEN go through it again.

Then start where you think you should start at.
Make notes of the steps you need to take and the resources required.
Use notes to create a step by step way to implement particular ideas.
Once you've created **YOUR** system you will not go back to the original,

The first question to ask and answer is "Why is this being done?"
How does this align with where you want to get to?
What are the strategic implications of doing this?
Does this fit in with getting to your goal in the shortest and fastest time?
What would it be like if it were totally successful?
Define it - what is success for this project and how will you know?

Now brainstorm all the tasks are involved.
It's important not to go linear too fast with this.
By linear, I mean step one, step two, step three, and step four.
You end up cutting off options.
Plan step one, two, three, there is a specific step that might be four.
Start too quickly, other ways of doing one, two, three, may not appear.

The first third of a brainstorming session is easy, generate ideas.
The second third is a little bit more challenging.
Go through those ideas and see where they lead to.
Push to think a little outside the box, that's often where a big idea is!
That's where the most powerful way to get the project done fastest - is.

Most never get to that level and short-changing themselves.
A project takes longer and they also set themselves up to procrastinate.

The final brainstorming part is incredibly important.
 Once you've brainstormed a project put options in a line sequence.
Figure out what you've overlooked and everything becomes obvious.
Get tasks in order, add missing steps, lay out a task list for the project.

Once you've organized the tasks into a linear process decide:
What things can you start immediately?

Step one is to start with no dependency on things to occur before.
There may be five, six or more steps that don't rely on anything else.
You can get started on them right away!

Write things you think of at the time, cross them off as done.
Add in stuff that is relevant from time to time.

MY FOCUS

I have taken many years to learn lessons and develop materials.
Look elsewhere but will not find solutions such as I offer.
Some may even sound similar but they WILL be different.
I doubt if others have the individual components.
Nor philosophic orientation.
Many who are not familiar with what I write may not realize that.

I want to imply a role like that used by a sports coach.
The best changes, improve or otherwise modifies behaviour.
The best coach has a basic understanding each student is different.

Display Art is non-cultural.
Any culture, speaking any language, can experience Display Art.
There is **NO** group or individual who cannot use this program.
You don't need a lot of **DISPLAY ART** to see results.

CREATIVITY
An expressive act from divergent + convergent thinking
Is creativity.

Years ago I had a 'Eureka' moments which you may have heard of.
I was demonstrating an art lesson to teachers.
Some stopped listening to me and became involved in what they dd.
That's when I made a startling and unexpected discovery.
The teachers were exhibiting creativity!

I'd read about creativity, creativeness and similar ideas.
I had some ideas about what creativity was.
Invention of new knowledge!

Creativity is a behaviour that is intrinsic to both art and education.
It is **NOT** language based!

Non-verbal education ought to be before any based on language.
Because that's actually how we learn (everything).
After we know something we can start finding words for that knowledge.

SKILL
Developed by repetition of a behaviour over a period of time.
It is necessary to build from situations where the behaviour is limited.
Creativity is a behaviour, so like any other behaviour skill can develop.
People considered creative possess that skill.

What about high level autonomous creativity?
Performance of a task is related to practice at that task.
With practice comes control and we can predict what might happen.
Practice even more we are increasingly effective, and results are better.
Creative people work at this level as a result of years of experience.

But developing skill takes a lot of time.
All children solve problems for that's how they learn to talk and walk.
Adult learning tends to be impatient and not allow time to develop skill.

The sport of body building illustrates what should take place.
The athlete completes many lifts over a lengthy period of time.
Small increments of additional weight are applied at regular intervals.
Eventually a weight-lifter builds sufficient strength to lift heavy weights.
Impossible weights at the beginning of the training process.

Developing skilled creativity is no different!
Many repetitions with interest and motivation = skill development.
It is necessary to build from situations where limited creativity operates.

Display Art is not rocket science but common sense.
Instead of a few seeming to be creative all students are.

But it has also been tested in real life.
Display Art works because it is right.
The thinking and the practice are in harmony.

THE REAL TEST
Success is measured by creativity development of students.
That also is the **ONLY** way to measure your coaching success.

BUT it's not me that will build your coaching skill for you.
To get **ANY** benefit from my ideas you must actually **DO** something!
There is very little gained by merely reading my material.

INDEX: DISPLAY ART

1. Display suggestions.

What not to do.
Try this.

What NOT to do.

Individual display in a group is NOT worthwhile.
Instead select **ONE** sample from each experiment.
Ideally select in alphabetical order or similar objective criteria.
A student may decline to display.

All other work is taken home or discarded.
The discarded works can be used for a group display (see this book).

Arrange the selected work immediately before the next lesson.
Other works are added in a similar fashion over a period of time.
Eventually all students are represented.

This avoids direct comparisons between individual student woks.
As in each case a different combination of materials was used.
All students are reminded of their own previous experiences too.
That's because of the same common materials.

Some advantages
No student work is displayed against wishes.
Adult opinion is unknown.
Enthusiasm is maintained and self-confidence developed.
No external standards set, so each student develops their own values.

No student can fail.
The situation is objective, non-competitive and thus non-threatening.

Wall space is used economically.

Mother is saved from an annual inspection of countless works.

2. Try this approach.

Make a large composite group piece.
Collect old discarded experiments and join them together.
Paste, pin, tape, staple or otherwise join and overlap the products.
Some may even be changed by altering the shape.

Thus NO individual work can be recognised in the final display.
Over-lapping and editing destroys individual original components.
Thus students discarding work avoid potential embarrassment.
They are still involved.
But memories of experiences stay in their mind for a very long time.

Hang the group work in a prominent place.
It may be added to from time to time.

Assemble each group display at a convenient time.
Sometimes the experiment time is expanded to include this activity.
But display could be time-consuming so other times are preferred.

There is an opportunity for themed group activity.
Themes can link other curriculum areas.
They are then meaningful and relevant ways to do this.
This is **MUCH** better than an "art" lesson focus.
On an objective from a different discipline!

Some advantages:

Worthwhile.
Use is made of products judged by a student to be unsuccessful.
Rejected material becomes part of an environment enhancing display.

The concept of re-cycling is introduced.
Students have an attractive environment with bigger displays.
There is also greater impact than usual.

Maintains student enthusiasm.

3. Your vision.

An approach to self-generated creativity.

It is tough to sit down in front of a blank page or screen and say,
"Okay, I'm going to create,"

You can't think about anything except what you're going to write.
You can't think about how much pressure you have.
You can't think about how much money is involved.

Now, how can you free yourself of all this anxiety?
All this blockage?
All this self-doubt?

It's very simple, of course.
What you do is use an old Zen trick.
Zen masters are enormously proficient, and have been for 2,000 years.
They have a very simple system which you can use every day.

You walk into the same place that you always write at.
At home or at the office, I happen to work at home.
I don't write any place else in the world except one desk.
It's where I've written for the past 38 years.

That desk is a nice, big, comfortable desk.
Come in at a set time that you may or may not keep.
I never keep it but it's somewhere around 9:30.
It's usually ten o'clock, but I know I'm going to be there every morning.

I come in, and you do the same thing all the time.
Many people sharpen pencils.
I have one cup of coffee in the morning, and that's my coffee for a day.
I take the coffee and I place it down but it will get cold.

I open my computer, and bring up the file I'm working on.
It's wonderful that it does that.
There's fifty pages staring at me, from page one.

But there is absolutely no necessity for me to work on the copy.
I can sit there.
I can stare.
I can drink the coffee.
I can stare some more, drink some more coffee.
I can do anything in the world except not get up from the desk.

So I just sit there.
But sooner or later, I'll get bored.
My boredom comes in one or two minutes.

Then, I begin looking at the copy.
As I look at the copy, I begin paging up and down.
As I do that, something reaches out from that computer and grabs me.
It says, "Hey, start with me."

I say:
Okay, this is good, but it's not quite great.
Wouldn't it be better if we just took these two words out?
Then condensed it a little?"

So, I do that!
Then, I go a little bit more and I see something else, so I do that.

I had no goal that has anything to do except for the copy.
And what is staring me in the face.
So, I'm not worried about anything!
Not money, the overhead, the rent, the new car or the new painting.
That's all gone and I'm just working on the copy.

Now, what I do is I work.
I am so absorbed that I don't notice the time passing.

But when I'm finished.
I am going to interrupt myself and do anything I want.
Maybe just scratch my head – do anything I want for five minutes.
Why?

Because when you're working, you're not creating.
The whole secret is to know when you're working.
Then leave work and go on to creation.
What do I mean by that?

Editing is not written for it really is stuff assembled.
You are working with a series of building blocks.
You are putting the building blocks together.
And then you are putting them in certain structures.
You are assembling images, and desires people might pay for.

To write poetry, prose, novels, or literature, avoid advertising.
Words in advertising are like the windows in a store.
You must be able to look right through them and see the product.

If you see the window, it's dirty.
You're going to see yourself or you're going to see the smear.
But you're not going to see the product.

Copy should never call attention to itself.
You should never know you are reading sentences.
The words should never pronounce themselves.
What you want people to see is the image of what the words convey.

You've got to break the fascination of needing the right words.
But when the right words come, the people don't see them.
They feel them.

Here an example using four words.
None of them is an exceptional word.
They're all pretty standard, mundane words.
Sneaky Little Arthritis Trick.
It is the combination that makes their power.

One of the words is a word that should not be used in advertising.
"Sneaky," because we don't like to sneak around.
When people sneak around is not very appealing.
You don't want to be identified with that.

A person with arthritic pain, humiliation and dependency.
Sees "Sneaky Little Arthritis Trick."
They've gone to doctors and spent hundreds of hours.
Just trying to follow them.
And still not been helped by doctors.
They know exactly what you're talking about.
It isn't at all like what it is when you were alone.

I assume that you're alone when you're writing, or working.
I'm alone.

Now, what am I doing when I do that?
I'm following what somebody else has done.
Somebody else organized some material and presented it in their way.
They may not know the market as well as I know the market.
They may not have the same experience as I do.

But they are setting up a sequence.
They are setting up a vocabulary, and they are setting up a tone.
It's all beautiful, but they're not going to sell the book.

You can do the same with this display program!

4. I hate words like creativity.

What does creativity mean?
Creativity is the ability to take two ideas that already exist.
They may be in two different sentences or even in two different fields.
You put them together and connect them.

What you do when creating is try to connect two separate ideas.
That logically would not go together up until that moment.

So, you're looking for a connection.
You're looking for a brand new connection.

When you have a brand new word connection.
You have something you can startle a reader with.
It might even stop your reader, or inspire, move or sell to your reader.

People leave doctors when they can't help them.
When doctors can help them, of course they stay with them.
They do the same with anyone!

5. Creativity is natural.

It is built into you by billions of years of evolution.
The only thing that makes creativity hard is:
We don't really know how to be quite clear about it.
We don't really know how to become connected.
So, we say:

How do we emerge from the conscious to the unconscious mind?
The conscious mind doesn't mean anything.
The unconscious mind doesn't mean anything either!
Maybe except mystic things.
That doesn't do us much good though.

It's better to refer to the focused mind and the unfocused mind.
The mind is a huge network of cells which retain thoughts or images.
It translates the images and thoughts back and forth.

The mind has vast networks of these cells.
It specializes in using only a certain amount of cells at a particular time.
Like when you looked at something – if you look right there.
You can only see this part of the room, and not the rest of the room.
This is quite in focus and the rest is blurred.

The brain connects when it plays.
When it thinks, uses logic, etc.
But if it doesn't connect, it doesn't make these connections.
The best example of I've seen, is the movie Amadeus about Mozart.

Mozart was a very unusual man, died at 32 I think.
He never rewrote his music.
Look at his scores, every note is put in place, and was never changed.
It's though he just wrote it from God and then sent it out to be played,
But it wasn't.

He had a simple system of escaping his focused conscious mind.
Everywhere he went he always had a billiard table available.
He'd also have a pen and his score, as well as the billiard table.

He would also have a cue ball.
He would take the white cue ball in his left hand.
He'd throw it out until it hit one, two, three sides and came back to him.

He'd catch it as it came back, pick it up, and throw it out, again.
And it would come back.
As it went on its little journey through the three sides, he wrote a note.
Then, he picked it up, threw again, wrote the note while it was traveling.
He picked it up and wrote one note at a time every three times it hit.

Why did he do this?
It was very simple.

If you throw a billiard ball out onto three of the sides.
The sides are soft enough that they'd randomize the billiard ball.
It would move very slightly.
So it doesn't come out a in predictable trajectory.

Your conscious mind changes direction as it goes out.
And you can't turn it into an unconscious mind.
A focused mind becomes trapped in watching that billiard ball.

Your unfocused mind can thus use its entire range.
To furnish you with the notes you're looking for.
That's if you're Mozart.

This is what we do when we think creatively.

6. Who are you writing to?

This is a very important question, absolutely essential.
Are you writing to a man?
Are you writing to a woman?
Are you writing to an individual or both sexes?
Are you writing to a mass audience?

What is your audience for this?
Unless you know and can answer that question.
You can't really direct what you write.

The answer is very simple, but two phased.
You're writing to an individual.
A single person always.
BUT they share a problem or desire with a huge mass of other people.

Try to identify the problem with the person reading what you write.
Which leads you to the most powerful word in the English language.
The most powerful word is not yes, and it's not free.
It's YOU.

That word YOU is critical.
In mail order publishing and mail order marketing.

It's just as important if you want someone to read what you write.
For example "Take the hands and apply the cream to the face."
BUT there are no the hands, and there is no the face.
There is only your hands and your face.

The first thing to do if those things are there, is change them.
Change all the "the's" into "you's" or "yours".

Also use as many terms as possible that people are familiar with.
BUT writing has to be full of you's.
AND
That you has to be one the reader can identify with.
You must be the person who writes like that.

Success is extremely lonely.
If you want to be successful, you have to accept the loneliness.

In addition:
You must accept extreme modesty and humbleness success demands.

I'll tell you why.
You have to know the person that you're going to ask for something.
Whether you're a salesman, a lawyer, or a judge, or whomever.
You have to know that person.

There's only one way you can learn that.
The greatest asset after hard work is the ability to listen.

You must listen to several different layers to be successful.
You have to listen first of all to the person who has whatever you've got.
They understand the problem you're going to try and solve.
You have to know that person so well that you can sound like him.
He will mistake you for his mirror image.

You also have to know the kind of society that he comes from.
Even the layer of society he comes from.
Your job is to ask questions, show appreciation and listen.

Basically you have to know society.
When you go to a party, or when you get in a taxi cab.
When you're with somebody on a bus or a subway,

7. Can groups be creative?

There are three stages generally proposed.

Stage 1: Individual ideas generation
Individual idea generation (divergent process)

In this stage users generate ideas individually.
To improve the quantity of idea generation.

When they are satisfied, or when that stage is over.
Users select a maximum of 5 ideas to share with other group members.

Stage 2: Incubate and generate more
All ideas selected by each user at the end of stage 1.
Are pooled and shown to all users.
Users can spend some time going through all ideas.
Then they can generate more ideas individually.

Only a subset of the best ideas is shared to the other members.
This way we reduce the amount of information.
It also make users reflect on their ideas.

To select the most promising 5 ideas (convergent process).
Share ideas and individual idea generation.
        (incubation + divergent process)
Select most promising 5 ideas from total of shared ideas.
        (convergent process)
Evaluated is the next stage

In the second stage users can see all the shared ideas.
They reflect on the shared ideas and continue to generate new ones.
Exposure to others' ideas followed by an incubation period.
This is mentally stimulating.
So there is a mix of individual generation with group stimulation.

At the end of this stage all select favourite 5 ideas from the total.
The pool of ideas are shared ideas + new generated ideas.

Again, users are asked to reflect on the ideas.
The final selection stage only the most promising ideas.
This reduces the final selection stage to a reasonable number of ideas.

Stage 3: Final evaluation
Final share of ideas (divergent process)
Select the best idea(s) (convergent process)

In this stage, ideas selected by each group member are pooled.
Users select the best idea (or a number of ideas).
They use the most suitable selection method.

So this group brainstorming method is a three stage process.
Each containing both a divergent and a convergent stage.
They go from problem definition to the selection of the best ideas.

The third stage is more than just a final selection.
Here users see for the first time ideas other group members generated.
They have been evaluated as worthwhile during the second stage.

Individuals generate as many ideas as they can at any time.
Unconventional ideas are welcome.
But users are required to reflect carefully on their own and others ideas.

This technique was developed to create a framework.
Which could be used to improve group brainstorming.
Quantity breeds quality **BUT**
Excessive quantity leads to information overload and decision paralysis.

Successful creativity is as random as possible to generate ideas.
But then the focus is on looking for the best ideas among them.
When you want to hit the target, you take aim carefully.
Good dart players don't throw at random hoping to hit the centre!

The process is anonymous.
Participants are free to write and select ideas without fearing evaluation.
Users don't need to brainstorm at the same time and in the same room.
They can be in different parts of the world and work at their own pace.

There is no production blocking.
Participants generate ideas without being distracted.
Other people speak and thus divide attention.

Each participant organises ideas on their own screen or paper.
They just do as they like best.
There is no more information overload.
Participants share only their most promising ideas.

Exposure to other ideas can give increased associative thinking.
That is the ability to generate more ideas.

Idea incubation also happens.
That's when participants are lead to reflect upon their and others' ideas.

Randomness may also spark creativity.
But focusing is needed to make sense and crystallise ideas.
Anonymity reduces evaluation apprehension.

8. Cultural differences

Coach Creativity Skill (the book) is non-cultural.
The materials used are common.
So little expenditure is required beyond usual expectations.

There is no judgment about any culture or group.
Students and coaches (teachers, parents, leaders) in any culture.
Speaking any language, can experience Coach Creativity Skill.
That's because culture is not an aspect of Coach Creativity Skill.

Some lower socio-economic groups are often action-oriented.
Coach Creativity Skill provides opportunities for this.
The activity is the base for affective and cognitive development growth.
Students are under no pressure to go beyond their own capabilities.

Migrants are often members of disadvantaged groups.
Language is usually an area of difficulty.
Coach Creativity Skill is primarily a non-language program.
But it can still develop innate thinking and problem-solving ability.

Coach Creativity Skill strategies and sequenced experiences:
Mean all students benefit.
There is improved self-discipline too.

Thinking divergently and convergently is successfully done.
So confidence built.

Self-evaluation is developed.
The ability to confidently make choices is enhanced.
A capacity to effectively cope with change is developed.
There are increased levels of mental health.

All students develop a sense of personal worth.

9. Was van Gogh substandard?

His paintings didn't sell whilst he was alive.
Have they changed since?
Now they bring astronomical prices.
But the paintings are still the same as the day they were done.
If "bad" in Vincent's day you would suppose they are still "bad".

But what has changed is people's opinion rather than the works.
Opinion is something that astute marketing can and should influence.
That's one of the roles of marketing.

An artist instead of blaming a painting for its failure to sell.
Should question the marketing.
Perhaps there was a failure to influence people's opinion?
Possibly a failure to even find out what opinions were held to start with?

People enter most buying situations with flexible buying criteria.
For example when you shop.
Whether for a lawyer, accountant, mattress, or most items or services.

How specific is your 'decision-making' criteria?
Just how expert are you in those areas?
Probably not much of an expert at all!

It is possible to re-set peoples' buying criteria.
Therein is an extraordinary opportunity.
Most people do not have a clue about most things they buy!

That applies to assembling classes too!
Potential students don't have sophisticated learning criteria.
They only know what they may have received in the past.

So you can re-set learning criteria for your intended student group.
Make your classes their most logical choice.
At the same time you might even gain the best financial result.
All without changing what you teach!

An example illustrates the effect of changing the buying criteria.
Some years ago Domino's Pizza stated 'we deliver pizza in 30 minutes. If less it is free' (they still do).

Effectively this claim changed the buying criteria for pizza.
Delivery speed became the main criteria!
It's a change that earned the pizza franchise many million $$$ since.

What s the buying criteria for your classes?

10. Art Education

Art Education is NOT the same as art.
Art education is art in an educational context.
It is art for educational purposes.
Art education must be justified educationally.

Thus art education is only a part of that which is art.
Similarly art education is not the sum of all that is educational.

There is a case for other educational areas.
They can deal with the remainder of the educational spectrum.
They will be differently educational in their objectives.

There may be overlapping.
Of some aspects of one with various aspects of another.
But this still doesn't make the two the same.

Art in elementary school is somewhat different from high school.
Certainly different from art in a tertiary level institution.
The former levels have development of the child as a prime concern.
Whilst this might also apply in relation to the student at the latter level.
There could also be vocational objectives.
The student is learning how to become an artist for example.

If it is believed that the business of art in education is to educate.
Educational ideas ought to be considered rather than artistic practices.
Pupil behaviour derived from understanding the essential nature of art.
According to educational criteria, ought to be paramount.

Behaviour of any kind only occurs in the course of some action.
Art education is concerned with the quality of the process (behaviour).
Rather than the production of objects.
As the essential behaviour of art is creativity.
Then that should be the focus of art education.

Awareness of creativity's central role is important for education.
The role of art education as a medium for creativity education is critical.

Various methods are used for achieving this objective.
All ought to be practical, realistic and workable.
It should be possible to provide individual tuition.
Within a group so pupils move to independence according to need.

WHERE NEXT:

Here is another book about developing creativity.
http://www.amazon.com/dp/B088T1KFQZ

NOT NOW:

These links take you to other books that might interest you:

What about your own memories?
YOU could publish them – like I did!
To find out how just get this book.
http://www.amazon.com/dp/B087DWKPTP

Starting an art career NOW is harder than it ever was.
To learn what to do - download this book.
http://www.amazon.com/dp/B088T7VJ76

Copying is the way most people start to become an artist!
To learn how - download this book.
http://www.amazon.com/dp/B088Y1DPL6

You could be interested in some more of my memories.
Find out what they are - buy this book.
http://www.amazon.com/dp/B088Y4RPL9

SEND TO:

Anyone interested in chocolate recipes?
Can download a book.
http://www.amazon.com/dp/B0882HK9Q9

Are you a parent, teacher or someone who meets a group regularly?
A simple way to start developing creativity is by displaying things.
To learn exactly how – buy this book.
http://www.amazon.com/dp/B088T1KFQZ

APPENDIX:

CAREER SUMMARY:
Summary of creative enterprises commenced:
Founder Riverina Galleries, Wagga Wagga 1979 - 1997.
Founder of Riverina Framing (from 1980-90).
Developed ArtPak a correspondence course for artists (1995)
Published 'Art Professional' newsletters for artists.
Author "SPACE Art Education" for primary schools NSW (1970 - 1982).

Summary of creative enterprises commenced with others:
Art consultant with NSW Department of Ed. from 1970-77 (Sydney).
Founder NSW Art Education Association (1970)
Art consultant with NSW Department of Ed. from 1980-81 (Riverina).
Consultant curator Charles Sturt University (1985-94).
Partner in Business Thinking Systems, Wagga Wagga (1999-2004).

Summary of related activity:
Graduate Bathurst Teachers College (1955).
Graduate National Art School (1970) distinctions ALL final year subjects
Graduate Macquarie University (1979)
Taught general studies, art, art education, art philosophy.
In pre-school, infants, primary, secondary, university adult education.
2 works hung Wynne Prize (1969) (major Australian landscape award).
Won various art awards and had 22 one-man exhibitions.
Judged art shows in various parts of Australia.
Writes in 'Australian Artist' magazine each month, since 1995.
Writes in 'International Artist' magazine each two months, since 2002.
Wrote 'Coaching Creative Hockey' published NSW Sport & Rec. (1974)
Coached Parkes Magpies, Parkes, Sydney University, University NSW.
Selector Parkes, Sydney, NSW hockey.
Deputy President NSWHA.
Founder MG Car Club of Wagga Wagga.
Founder Gathering of the Faithful MG Car Club of Wagga Wagga.

www.ingramcontent.com/pod-product-compliance
Lightning Source LLC
Chambersburg PA
CBHW030541220526
45463CB00007B/2932